BRITISH COLUMBIA

JOURNEY ACROSS CANADA

Harry Beckett

The Rourke Book Co., Inc.
Vero Beach, Florida 32964

© 1997 The Rourke Book Co., Inc.

Harry Beckett M.A. (Cambridge), M.Ed. (Toronto), Dip.Ed. (Hull, England) has taught at the elementary and high school levels in England, Canada, France, and Germany. He has also travelled widely for a tour operator and a major book company.

Edited by Laura Edlund
Laura Edlund received her B.A. in English literature from the University of Toronto and studied Writing for Multimedia and Book Editing and Design at Centennial College. She has been an editor since 1986 and a traveller always.

ACKNOWLEDGMENTS
For photographs: Geovisuals (Kitchener, Ontario), The Canadian Tourism Commission and its photographers.
For reference: *The Canadian Encyclopedia, Encarta 1997, The Canadian Global Almanac, Symbols of Canada. Canadian Heritage*, Reproduced with the permission of the Minister of Public Works and Government Services Canada, 1997.
For maps: Promo-Grafx of Collingwood, Ont., Canada.

Library of Congress Cataloging-in-Publication Data

Beckett, Harry. 1936 -
    British Columbia / by Harry Beckett.
        p. cm. — (Journey across Canada)
    Includes index.
    Summary: Discusses the geography, climate, industries, people, culture, and major cities of Canada's westernmost province.
    ISBN 1-55916-206-6
    1. British Columbia—Juvenile literature. [1. British Columbia.]
I. Title II. Series: Beckett, Harry, 1936 -   Journey across Canada.
F1087.4.B43 1997
971.1—dc21   97–13887
                                                       CIP
                                                       AC

Printed in the USA

TABLE OF CONTENTS

Size and Location 5

Geography: Land and Water 6

What Is the Weather Like? 8

Making a Living: Harvesting the Land 11

From the Earliest Peoples 12

Making a Living: From Industry 14

If You Go There 17

Major Cities 18

Signs and Symbols 20

Glossary 23

Index 24

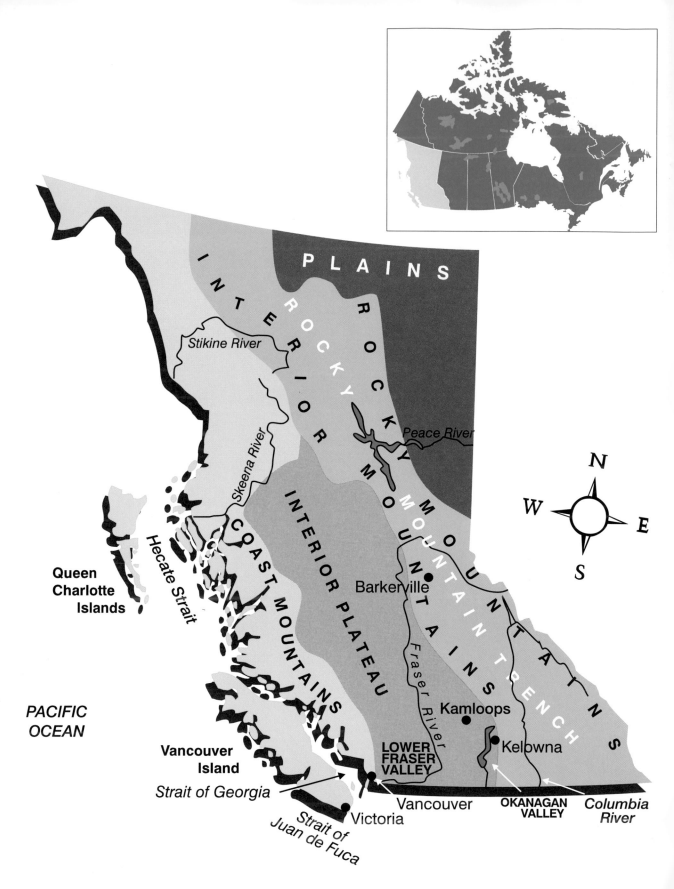

PLAINS

INTERIOR

Stikine River

ROCKY

Peace River

Skeena River

Queen Charlotte Islands

Hecate Strait

COAST MOUNTAINS

INTERIOR PLATEAU

Barkerville

MOUNTAINS

TRENCH

Fraser River

PACIFIC OCEAN

Kamloops

Kelowna

Vancouver Island

Strait of Georgia

LOWER FRASER VALLEY

Vancouver

OKANAGAN VALLEY

Columbia River

Strait of Juan de Fuca

Victoria

N
W *E*
S

PROVINCE OF BRITISH COLUMBIA

Chapter One

SIZE AND LOCATION

British Columbia, or B.C., is Canada's westernmost province and the third largest. It is 947 800 square kilometres (365 974 square miles) in area, including the islands off the west coast.

From north to south it runs 1250 kilometres (777 miles) from the Yukon and Northwest Territories to the states of Washington, Idaho, and Montana. From west to east in the southern portion of the province, B.C. extends from the Pacific Ocean to the Rockies bordering Alberta. Farther north, it extends from the Alaska **Panhandle** (PAN han dul) to the 120th line of **longitude** (LON jih tood) west.

On the Pacific coast, many **fiords** (fyordz) and inlets cut into the mainland. The Queen Charlotte Islands, Vancouver Island, and others lie off the coast, separated from the mainland by **straits** (STRAYTS).

Find out more...

- The highest point is Mount Fairweather, at 4663 metres (15 299 feet) high, on the border with Alaska.
- Three major straits are Hecate Strait, the Strait of Georgia, and the Strait of Juan de Fuca.

5

Chapter Two

GEOGRAPHY: LAND AND WATER

Except in the Vancouver area and the northeastern corner of the province, most of British Columbia is mountainous. On the mainland, the major groups of mountains are the Rocky Mountains, the Interior Mountains, and the Coast Mountains. There are also mountains on the islands.

The Rockies are high and jagged in the south, but lower and more rounded in the north.

Lake O'Hara in Yoho National Park in the Rocky Mountains

The Okanagan Valley in the interior is less mountainous and quite dry.

To their east is the Rocky Mountain Trench, a long valley. Next come the ranges that make up the Interior Mountains, followed by the Interior Plateau, which is forested upland. Finally on the mainland, there are the Coast Mountains. These are lower in the south than in the north.

Three of the province's major rivers—the Fraser, Skeena, and Stikine—cut through the Coast Mountains. The province is named for the Columbia River, in southeastern B.C.

Chapter Three

WHAT IS THE WEATHER LIKE?

The mountains give British Columbia a varied climate. The biggest climate differences are between the coast and the province's interior.

The coast has mild, wet winters and moderate, drier summers. From October to April, moist winter weather brings heavy **precipitation** (prih sip ih TAY shun) to western Vancouver Island and the mainland coast. As the winds climb the mountain slopes, they cool. Cold air cannot hold its moisture content so drops the moisture as rain or snow.

The interior, on the other side of the mountains, receives dry air, low precipitation, and more extreme temperatures.

The climate also varies from north to south. Air from Alaska and the Yukon makes winters cold in the northeast.

Vancouver's early spring blossoms

Find out more...

• Average temperatures in Vancouver are 2.5°C (36.5° F) in January, but 17.3°C (63.1° F) in July.

• Vancouver gets about 1167 millimetres (46 inches) yearly precipitation. The southern Okanagan Valley gets only 300 to 400 millimetres (12 to 16 inches).

8

Chapter Four

MAKING A LIVING: HARVESTING THE LAND

British Columbia is rich with natural **resources** (rih ZORS iz)—excellent farmland, large forests, and a fishing industry.

Farmers make good use of the farmland. There is **livestock** (LIVE stok), dairy, and crop farming in the fertile Lower Fraser Valley, cattle ranching on the grassland plateaus of the southern interior, and grain growing in the Peace River area.

Forestry is B.C.'s largest resource industry. It started on Vancouver Island in the 1840s. Trees were plentiful and the lumber could be transported by water. Since then logging has been done on the mainland, including in the interior.

Fishing is another major industry. Fish are caught both off the coast and at river mouths. Recently the number of salmon has shrunk.

These log booms were brought to the sawmill in Victoria by water.

Find out more...

- Thanks to irrigation, the Okanagan Valley has become known for its fruit and vegetables.
- Now some people are concerned that the forests are used too much.

Chapter Five

FROM THE EARLIEST PEOPLES

The Native peoples of the northwest coast—including the Haida (HY duh)—were fishers, hunters, and gatherers. They lived in large, settled family groups on the salmon rivers. Those in the interior—such as the Kootenay (KOO tuh nay)—travelled from place to place for food.

Europeans came first for furs, and starting in 1858, to join the Fraser River Valley Gold Rush.

A meeting of cultures, Native and British

Many Native people still earn their living from fishing.

Chinese immigrants worked in the mines and at building the Canadian Pacific Railway. In the southern interior, towns grew around mining and forestry. But most newcomers came to the Lower Mainland, with its mild climate. The arrival of the railway in Vancouver gave easy access from the east.

Once known for its Britishness, the province now reflects many cultures, particularly Asian, in its streets and neighbourhoods.

Chapter Six

MAKING A LIVING: FROM INDUSTRY

British Columbia's manufacturing is based on its natural resources.

Manufacturers use wood to produce building lumber, pulp, and paper. Salmon and farm produce are canned; grapes are made into wine.

Mining provides coal, natural gas, and oil, which are **processed** (PROS est) to produce energy and chemicals. The province also produces its own hydro-electricity.

Tourism is a major industry. The Rocky Mountains draw tourists from all over the world.

Transportation is difficult in this mountainous province, but important for all industries. Only four passes through the Rocky Mountains allow the many roads and the two national railways through.

Find out more...

- Some metals mined are gold, copper, molybdenum, and zinc.
- The new Coquihalla Highway has opened up Kelowna and Kamloops to tourists from the coast.

In a deep river valley, the Trans-Canada Highway and the Canadian Pacific Railway

Chapter Seven

IF YOU GO THERE...

British Columbia is an ideal destination for people who love nature and outdoor recreation.

National parks open up spectacular scenery to everyone. There is fishing, camping, and hiking on Vancouver Island and in the Rocky Mountains. A new park on the Queen Charlotte Islands has the most varied plant and animal life in North America. A Haida village in these islands is now a World Heritage Site.

North of Vancouver is the world-famous Whistler-Blackcomb ski resort. In the interior the Okanagan Valley offers skiing near Kelowna and camping all summer long.

Barkerville, also in the interior, is a restored gold rush town from the 1860s. It became a ghost town when no more gold could be found.

Skiing at Big White in the Okanagan

Find out more...

- The Haida village on Anthony Island is famous for its totem poles and longhouses.
- Barkerville's population once reached 25 000.

Chapter Eight

MAJOR CITIES

Victoria, the provincial capital, is on the southern tip of Vancouver Island. It has an international airport, and ferries link it with the mainland.

Called the City of Gardens, Victoria is known for its waterfront, old town, fine buildings, British character, and pleasant climate. The government and university are major employers.

The Parliament Buildings, seen across the Inner Harbour in Victoria

Family fun in a park in central Vancouver

Vancouver, the third biggest city in Canada and a leading Pacific seaport, is set against the magnificent backdrop of the Coast Mountains. It hosted the 1986 World Exposition, focussing on transportation and communication.

The old city district of Gastown has been restored, and Vancouver's Chinatown is one of the largest in North America. The city's Stanley Park has a zoo and an aquarium.

Chapter Nine
SIGNS AND SYMBOLS

The provincial flag shows the Union Jack and an antique crown to symbolize the province's British origins. The blue and white bars represent the Pacific Ocean, and the sun setting (in the west) reminds us of B.C.'s position as Canada's westernmost province.

On the coat of arms, the flag design is repeated. On either side, the wapiti deer and the bighorn sheep represent Vancouver Island and the rest of British Columbia. Above the shield is a golden helmet and two royal symbols, a crown and a lion. The ribbons show Canada's colours, red and white. The provincial flower appears around the lion's neck and below the motto.

The Latin motto means "Splendour without diminishment."

The floral emblem is the Pacific dogwood, a tree which blossoms in April and May.

British Columbia's flag, coat of arms, and flower

GLOSSARY

fiord (fyord) — a long, steep-sided inlet from the sea

Haida (HY duh) — a Native people living in the Queen Charlotte Islands

Kootenay (KOO tuh nay) — a Native people living near Kootenay Lake in southeastern B.C.

livestock (LIVE stok) — farm animals

longitude (LON jih tood) — distance east or west, shown on maps as lines from the North to South Pole

Panhandle (PAN han dul) — a narrow strip of land shaped like the handle of a pan

precipitation (prih sip ih TAY shun) — rain, dew, or snow

process (PROS es) — to prepare or treat using a special method

resource (rih ZORS) — something that can be used

strait (STRAYT) — a narrow water channel between two larger water bodies

Beautiful Butchart Gardens, Victoria

INDEX

climate   8, 13, 18

explorers and settlers
   12, 13

farming   11, 14

fishing   11, 12, 13,
   14, 17

forests   7, 11, 13, 14

islands   5, 6, 8, 17, 18

lakes and rivers   7, 11,
   12, 14

mining   12, 13, 14, 17

mountains   5, 6, 8, 14,
   17, 19

Native peoples
   12, 17

ocean   5, 20

tourism   14, 17

transportation
   13, 14, 18, 19

valleys   7, 8, 11,
   12, 17

Vancouver   6, 8,
   13, 19

Victoria   11, 18

wildlife   17, 20